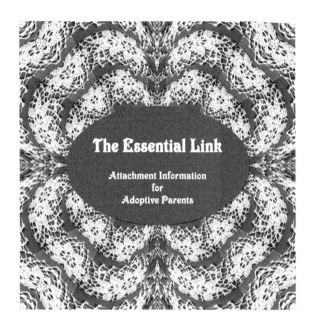

by Susan M. Ward

Carolina Mountain Counseling
and
Parent Support

www.carolinamountaincounseling.com

Asheville, North Carolina

**Published by Carolina Mountain Counseling
2013**

Carolina Mountain Counseling and Parent Support helps families with challenging children

> Visit my website at
> www.CarolinaMountainCounseling.com

© Copyright Susan Ward, 2013.
All rights reserved.
Printed in the United States of America
First Printing: 2001
Revised: 2003, 2006, 2008, 2013

No part of this book may be reproduced in any form or by any electronic or mechanical means including information storage and retrieval systems, without permission in writing from the author. The only exception is by a reviewer, who may quote short excerpts in a review.

ISBN: 1440410844
EAN-13: 9781440410840

Introduction

Attachment - creating a solid, trusting relationships between parent and child - is the core topic of this small book. The important nature of this bond has been acknowledged as critical to a child's development and mental well being since the 1950s and 1960s with the work of Dr. John Bowlby, trained in psychiatry and psychoanalysis.

"No variables have more far-reaching effects on personality development than a child's experiences within the family, wrote Dr. Bowlby. Starting during his first months in his relation to both parents, he builds up working models of how attachment figures are likely to behave toward him in any of a variety of situations, and on all those models are based all his expectations, and therefore all his plans, for the rest of his life." (*Attachment and Loss*, by John Bowlby, 1973)

Familiarity with attachment means adoptive parents will provide the proper environment for their children to form strong, lifelong attachments. Knowledge of attachment issues means that children who need additional parenting interventions will receive what they require. And, understanding attachment disorder means that children who need specialized therapy for attachment issues or reactive attachment disorder (RAD) will receive the therapy and parenting that they need to heal, become attached, and be productive family members.

As you read this book, you'll find suggestions and recommendations that apply to children adopted at any age. If you're adopting a baby, the nurturing activities and recommendations that apply to children adopted at any age. If you're adopting a baby, the nurturing activities that help your child feel safe and connected will be most relevant. If you adopt a toddler or older child, you'll also need to focus on establishing rules and implementing consequences. This book will also provide insights into the behaviors and healing of children with attachment disorder.

This book includes the words of attachment experts, as well as my own experiences. I've been a foster parent, attachment parenting specialist, and therapeutic tutor. And, over the past eleven years I've provided therapeutic respite for over 200 children, all diagnosed with attachment issues or reactive attachment disorder. Whether you are praying you won't adopt a child with attachment challenges, or are parenting a child diagnosed with RAD, I have been there, too. My child has healed from the early trauma that resulted in reactive attachment disorder and is now a healthy, successful young adult.

Do not dismiss the topic of attachment and assume that your child has the ability to attach easily and fully. Every single adopted child has some degree of attachment challenges. Educate yourself so that you can provide all that your child needs to meet their fullest potential.

The Essential Link provides you with basic awareness and preliminary guidance about this critical aspect of adoptive parenting. Implementing this information will help your child learn to trust, love, care, and be confident about their world.

Best wishes on your adoption journey!
Susan Ward

Attachment... the essential link,
cannot be ignored by anyone connected to the world of adoption

Forward

Attachment is fundamental to all human existence. The strength of each individual's attachment to their mother, their parents, their friends, and even their pets, establishes their ability to function well throughout their lives. Creating strong mutual attachment is the primary task of every adoptive parent.

Parents need to understand how attachments are created and how to create daily occurrences that will foster that attachment. Some children arrive into their adoptive families with the potential to become quickly and securely attached. Other children need additional interventions for attachment to occur.

This book, *The Essential Link: Attachment Information for Adoptive Parents*, provides adoptive parents of any age child with a summary of what attachment is and information to help you and your child become securely attached.

This topic cannot be overlooked by adoption agencies, parents, or adoptive personnel if our goal is to create happy, well functioning, families.

       Theresa Anderson, MA, LPC. Attachment therapist
               Burnsville, North Carolina

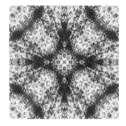

Attachment... the essential link starts even before birth

WHAT IS ATTACHMENT?

As an adoptive parent or adoptive parent-to-be, attachment is a word you read and hear about frequently. Attachment and bonding. Attaching to your new child. Strong attachments. Attachment issues. Reactive attachment disorder.

Attachment - the emotional connection between parent and child - is not uniform from child to child. It varies according to the child's history, personality, biological and neurological issues, and the parents' ability to parent.

Attachment falls along a continuum that includes many variations. At one end are children who have solid attachments. In the middle are children with attachment issues in need of interventions. At the far end are children with more severe attachment issues who may be diagnosed with reactive attachment disorder (RAD).

As an adoptive parent, think of attachment with your child like restoring an old house. If the foundation of the old house is solid and your examination doesn't uncover much damage, it may not take much time or money to repair it. If, over time, you realize the house has quite a list of problems, you'll have to dedicate more energy to making it a livable home. But, if the old house does not have a strong foundation, you'll need to dedicate resources to fixing the underpinnings of the house before you can even begin to work on fixing the interior.

Well-established attachment during a child's early years creates the groundwork for a child's future experiences, emotions, and successes. Attachment starts even before birth, impacted by the health, medical care, and state of mind of the mother-to-be. And when the child is born, attachment is shaped by the quality of the affection, care, feeding, attention, and touching that the child receives.

Attachment is also impacted by the child's health and neurology at birth, i.e., asthma, ear infections, premature birth, FASD (fetal alcohol spectrum disorder), sensory processing disorder, or other illnesses and disorders. Additionally, attachment is affected by the parents' health and ability to spend time with their child.

In *Adopting the Hurt Child*, Greg Keck, Ph.D., describes the bonding cycle. In a well-functioning family, he says, a baby learns that if he has a need, expressed by crying/frustration, someone will gratify that need, and the gratification leads to the development of his trust in others. This cycle of need, followed by anger/rage, followed by gratification, and followed by trust, is repeated thousands of times to form the foundation of life. "Without the successful completion of this cycle at some point, it is doubtful that an individual's growth will proceed normally without specific therapeutic intervention."

In *Bonding: Building the Foundations of Secure Attachment and Independence*, by Marshall H. Klaus et al, the authors describe early attachments by saying, "It is from this emotional connection that infants can begin to develop a sense of who they are and from which a child can evolve and be able to venture into the world. Without a secure base established in infancy, humans from childhood throughout adult life may develop and cling to the belief that the world is unstable, and that they cannot safely trust others."

Children who were adopted may have many of their connections, their bonds, their attachments, their ability to trust, weakened or broken. The attachments may be unstable, as in a child whose birth parent(s) gave intermittent quality care to their child due to illness or limited parenting skills. They may have been broken, as in a child who is removed from their birth family and in and out of foster homes or orphanages during the first three years of their life. Or, the child may not have attached at all to a primary caregiver due to situations of prenatal illness, newborn illnesses, or extreme neglect and/or abuse.

Notes... thoughts... questions to yourself

Is this what you thought attachment was about? What do you think is the likelihood that your child has or might have attachment challenges?

Attachment... is impacted by early life trauma

Trauma, the Brain, and Attachment

While there are numerous issues that can create attachment problems in a child, one of the more-recently understood and researched is the impact of trauma. Trauma can be exposure to horrific events, loss of a parent or sibling, or long-term neglect. Research over the past few years into the brain has provided many details about how the brain works, as well as how trauma can cause the brain to not function properly.

The functional capabilities of the mature brain develop throughout life, but the vast majority of critical structural and functional organization takes place in childhood. Indeed, by the age of three the brain has reached 90% of adult size, while the body is still only about 18% of adult size. By shaping the developing brain, experiences of childhood define the adult, explains Dr. Bruce Perry, the head of Child Trauma Programs in Houston, and Chief of Psychiatry at Texas Children's Hospital at Baylor College of Medicine.

Virtually all children with RAD or attachment issues have suffered from some level of trauma - the trauma that causes the attachment problems. For example, many

children who were adopted had been neglected by their birth families - not enough food, limited affection and attention from parents, lack of attending to the child's physical needs, untreated illnesses, and more. Each of these instances creates a sense of anxiety and/or fear in the child. Emotionally and psychologically, the child may lose their ability to trust and have difficulties with cause and effect. Neurologically, the child's traumatized brain does not develop the same as a child who lives in a nurturing environment. Dr. Bruce Perry states...
"Children reflect the world in which they are raised. If that world is characterized by threat, chaos, unpredictability, fear and trauma, the brain will reflect that by altering the development of the neural systems involved in the stress and fear response."

Trauma resulting in attachment problems can be mitigated or sometimes even erased with specialized parenting approaches and targeted therapies. Dr. Perry explains that some of the usual therapy approaches are ineffective when helping children deal with trauma: in effect, words are not enough.

> No matter how much you talk to someone the words will not easily get translated into changes in the midbrain or the brainstem. Once someone learns how to ride a bicycle the parts of the brain

involved in that action are indelibly altered -- they will always know how to ride a bicycle. No matter how often someone talks to you (cortical activity), the parts of the brain involved in motor memory will not change. No amount of talking can unlearn and change the part of the brain that is controlling the simple motor memories involved in riding a bicycle. You may learn to not get on bicycles or if you do get on bicycles to not put your feet on the pedals but you can not unlearn the motor behavior.

When helping a child recover from trauma and the resultant attachment challenges, a child needs multiple interventions, all wrapped within a nurturing environment. The major way to have impact on those primitive parts of the brain (is) to provide predictability, nurturance, support, and cognitive or insight oriented interventions which make a child feel safe, comfortable and loved, says Dr. Perry.

While attachment is considered the major challenge facing children exposed to trauma, other issues can arise including sensory processing disorder, auditory processing disorder, and many others. Once attachment is secure between parent and child, the need for adjunct therapies should be explored.

This quick reference to trauma, the brain, and attachment is meant to bring an awareness to the topic. As J. Douglas Bremner, M.D. says that posttraumatic stress disorder is 10 times more common than cancer, but our society spends only one-tenth as much for research on this disorder as it spends for cancer research. Parents should be aware of how critical trauma is on the development of our children's brains, emotions, and overall well being, and keep up with new discoveries into the brain.

Notes... thoughts... questions to yourself

Trauma and neglect? Had you thought about the impact that the trauma in your child's early life might have had?

Attachment... how to create the bond and connection

HOW TO FACILITATE ATTACHMENT

Whatever the level of attachment your child achieved before adoption, you need to create new attachments between yourself and your child. You need to foster an environment that helps your child feel secure, accepted, cared for, responded to, loved, and enjoyed. Additionally, a child needs to feel emotionally safe; to know that it's ok to have feelings, real feelings, even overwhelming feelings.

Attachment is not based on your instant love for a child when you meet them, nor on your feelings of total acceptance for the child, nor even a feeling that this child is meant to be yours. Attachment is your child's ability to engage with you in affectionate, willing, and positive ways. And your own ability to reciprocate in positive, resourceful ways.

Attachment takes time. It takes energy. It takes commitment on behalf of the parents. Your child, no matter what her age when she comes to live with you, is subjected to great stressors: new foods, new smells, new sounds, grief, sadness, loneliness, and more. It is the responsibility of parents to help the child to adjust and attach to her new family during this stressful time.

Fostering attachment includes encouraging appropriate dependence upon you as the primary caregiver. In many ways, you are recreating the bonding and attachment cycle that your child felt, or didn't feel, as a baby. That is, "By repeated assurance that emotional and physical needs will be met, the baby begins to develop a sense of basic trust." (*Bonding: Building the Foundations of Secure Attachment and Independence*, by Klaus)

You encourage attachment through minimizing your child's exposure to new people and activities during the early months; setting clear-cut rules from the beginning; not trying to be "easy" on your new child; by you, the parents (not your child) setting the emotional tone for the family; and by creating family traditions and rituals.

Nurturing activities are a requirement for parental-child attachment. Attachment is created through smiles, touch, motion, and food, the same basic ingredients for creating successful attachment during the first three years of a child's life. Actions and activities for babies include carrying, bottle or breast feeding, eye contact, snuggling, rocking, and laughing. For toddlers and older children bonding activities might include swimming together, singing songs, dancing together, massage, silly games, back rubs, cuddling, rocking, and reading together.

Dan Hughes, Ph.D., author of *Facilitating Developmental Attachment*, lists some nurturing activities in his chapter on day-to-day parenting. His list includes:

-Frequent eye contact and smiles

-Touch: long and short, tickles and hugs, loud and quiet, light and squeezed, rocking and snuggling, laughing and crying

-Meals with conversations about family and self interests

-Quiet bedtime rituals

-Music

-Photographs

-Cooking, reading, group chores and activities

-Child has role in family rituals and celebrations

-Helping child with skill development

Integration of these actions into your family's life creates the environment that your child needs to attach to you.

Parenting the Hurt Child, the 2009 book by Gregory Keck and Regina M. Kupecky, provides numerous tips for connecting to your child. Examples include jump rope together, play a clapping game, draw on each other with washable markers, mail your child a note, tell the story of your child's adoption again and again, and have a pajama party with the family. They say, "We often find that parents who are the most spontaneous, the most creative, the most unusual, the most unpredictable and therefore the most fun are the ones whose children finally "get it."

In addition to nurturing, children need to feel safe in order to trust their new parents. For babies, this means having their basic needs met on a consistent and regular basis. For toddlers and older children, safety is maintained through setting rules, providing consequences for breaking the rules, and limiting a child's choices. A child's safety, especially one who comes from a traumatic background, comes from us, the parents, staying in control and not letting them create emotional turmoil within the family.

One parenting approach, advocated by many adoption agencies, therapists, and family advocates, is called 'love and logic.' This parenting style was developed by Foster Cline, M.D., and Jim Fay. In the introduction of their book, *Parenting With Love and Logic*, they write, "Our approach is more of an attitude that, when carried out in the context of a healthy, loving relationship with our children, will allow them to grow in maturity as they grow in years. It will teach them to think, to decide, and to live with their decisions."

Cline and Fay fill their book with practical information and tips. One tip is called, "Messages that Lock in Love."

A lot of hugs, wrestling, friendly pushing and shoving, and even playful punching all forge a strong bond between parents and children. Blend these with smiles and eye contact. Use these emotional times to lock in implied messages such as:

-"You do a great job of thinking for yourself."

-"You are always a good helper when I need you."

-"There's always a lot of love here regardless of what happens."

-"It looks as if you will always be able to solve your own problems."

-"I bet you feel good when you do such a good job."

Over time, most children who were adopted, respond and properly attach to parents who understand the attachment process, and who provide the structure, guidance, and nurturing necessary for a child to feel safe. These securely attached children show empathy toward people and animals; interact in a mutual give and take with parents, siblings, and friends; have a conscience; show true affection; look into people's eyes when speaking; have a sense of self; are fairly flexible; show respect; understand boundaries; and have a genuine depth to all of their emotions.

Notes... thoughts... questions to yourself

Some parents assume that attachment just happens. Did you realize that it would take energy and effort on your part to help it occur? How many of these recommendations will be easy for you to implement? How many will be hard?

Attachment... the essential link, may be compromised in children by issues relating to trust, grief, abandonment...

WHEN ATTACHING NEEDS HELP

Hopefully, your child will arrive into her family with the ability to attach. With that ability intact, and your parenting skills attuned to fostering an attachment, your child should begin to connect to you, to trust you, to love you.

Most children who are surrounded by love, nurturing, and security will learn to trust and become attached. However, some children may need additional attachment interventions.

For example, because of being born into families who couldn't properly care for them, some children missed out on basic baby and toddler attachment activities. If your child missed these, fill in the gaps by re-parenting them: rock your child, sing lullabies, play toddler games, i.e., patty cake, feed her baby food, and hold her while giving her a bottle no matter what her chronological age is. Your child may need this extra level of nurturing in order to attach to you.

An older child may need to be parented as if a toddler in order to learn to trust you and feel safe. This might include keeping your child within eyesight, limited choices regarding toys, privileges appropriate to a toddler, and lots of "mom" (or "dad") time. Have them play near you while you pay bills. Let them help you with your chores. They may not be ready to be treated like their chronological age, but rather their emotional age. By doing this, you're helping them learn from you how parents and children interact, love, and trust each other.

Despite proper attachment parenting, some children may not fully attach. They may be anxious, grief-filled, rage filled, or exhibit other ongoing behaviors and emotions that separate them from happy, confident, affectionate, attached children. These children most likely formed some level of bond and attachment to their caregivers in the past, but the attachments were broken. These children may have issues relating to trust, grief, abandonment, and behavior that need interventions. These types of attachment challenges are often aided by intensive nurturing activities at home. Or, they require short-term therapeutic interventions from an attachment therapist who can help the parents and child to fine-tune their attachment to each other.

But what if your child does not attach? What if you've added high-intensity nurturing activities, and your child still seems distant? What if your child has seen a therapist, and they still rage and defy you? What if you feel as if you have a 'hotel guest' staying with you? What if, despite your efforts, your child's attachment does not feel secure? What if your child continually rebuffs your affection? What if your child regularly ignores your directions? What if your child displays a lack of conscience? Does your child have RAD (reactive attachment disorder)?

Notes... thoughts... questions to yourself

Do you think your child has or will have slight attachment issues or might they end up being diagnosed with RAD? Have you spoken with other parents who have questions about attaching to their child?

WHAT DOES RAD LOOK LIKE?

All books on attachment disorder provide a slightly varying, yet similar list of RAD symptoms. Importantly, most of those books also describe how these symptoms are similar to other childhood disorders such as ADHD, bipolar, oppositional defiant disorder (ODD), and others.

As a starting point, consider the following partial list of RAD characteristics from *Toddler Adoption: The Weaver's Craft,* by Mary Hopkins-Best:

-Resistance to being comforted and cuddled
-Ambivalent behavior toward parents
-Scarcity of distinction between parents and strangers
-Raging and aggressive behavior
-Extremely negative and controlling behavior
-Unorganized behavior and poor impulse control

Toddler Adoption goes on to say, "It is when these characteristics are extremely resistant to change in spite of parenting efforts to develop attachment that they become indicative of a chronic and pervasive problems. Because attachment problems become more resistant to change as the child grows, early intervention is essential."

In addition to characteristics that a child with RAD may have, there are characteristics that the parents of attachment disordered children may have. The two most common parent traits are extreme frustration that no parenting techniques are working to modify their child's behavior, and exhaustion due to the pervasiveness of their child's inappropriate behaviors. At the same time, people outside the immediate family - grandparents, teachers, neighbors - are seldom exposed to your child's worst behaviors, which adds even more frustration to the parents' life. Even experienced therapists may not understand the depth of the challenges facing families who have a child with issues relating to early life trauma and attachment, if they are untrained in trauma and attachment.

Notes... thoughts... questions to yourself

Does your child exhibit any of these characteristics in the extreme? How are you feeling about your interactions with your child? Should you consider an outside assessment?

Attachment... the essential link, may be strong, shaky, or insecure when your child joins the family

WHAT IF IT IS RAD...?

Reactive attachment disorder is treatable for most children. However, time is NOT on your side. As with most disorders, the sooner the treatment and interventions begin, the more potential there is for your child to heal and develop into a productive, caring, responsible adult.

If you suspect that your child has serious attachment issues, or RAD, find an attachment therapist. Many, many parents arrive at an attachment therapist's office after having tried several other therapists unfamiliar with treating RAD. One mom to a nine-year-old in Ohio said, "My world changed when we found an attachment therapist. Suddenly, I was being supported. My son's rages and controlling behaviors (that few people saw outside our home) were not considered acceptable. My son was forced to confront himself. My son finally began to heal."

As you search for an attachment therapist, find one who is familiar with other similar and sometimes interrelated disorders such as PTSD, autism, ADD, ADHD, bipolar, FASD, etc., or who has partnerships with other therapists to assist with related disorders. Talk to other parents of children with RAD and find out what support systems they have in place. They may be able to direct you to local support groups and respite providers.

If your child is diagnosed with RAD, she will need therapy, AND therapeutic parenting. A child with RAD needs to be enveloped in a package of therapeutic interventions. This wraparound care helps your child improve their understanding of cause and effect; breaks down the fears in your child; creates a solid bond with you the parent; lets you, the parent be in charge; encourages the grieving that your child needs to do; and helps your child rewrite her view of herself.

Therapeutic parenting provides a super consistent, extra empathetic, very supportive, highly structured, extremely nurturing environment for children for whom traditional parenting approaches do not work. Children helped by therapeutic parenting may suffer not only from reactive attachment disorder (RAD), but bipolar disorder, Tourette's Syndrome, PTSD, ODD, attention deficit disorder, hyperactivity, and other challenging behaviors.

Two of the experts of therapeutic parenting are Nancy Thomas and Daniel Hughes. Nancy Thomas is a therapeutic parenting specialist who has worked with many severely emotionally disturbed children. Daniel Hughes is a psychologist who specializes in child abuse and neglect, and attachment disordered children. Both Dr. Hughes and Ms. Thomas emphasize the need to balance high expectations and consequences, with lots of love, attention, and nurturing.

Nancy Thomas says that children, no matter what their disability or limitations, should learn to be respectful, responsible, and fun to be around. She teaches parents to create a system where children are given clear expectations, choices, rewards, and consequences.

Similarly, Dan Hughes explains how parents need to maintain an accepting, empathetic, loving, curious, and playful attitude, no matter how challenging the behavior of the child. He also advocates, as does Nancy Thomas, a very structured routine, and encourages unpredictable consequences for misbehaviors.

Attachment, Trauma, and Healing, by Terry M. Levy and Michael Orlans, discusses parenting children diagnosed with RAD:

"Although all parenting is a challenging (and rewarding) task, parenting the child with attachment disorder is especially arduous. These children are commonly mistrustful, angry, irresponsible, defensive, dishonest, destructive, and do not give or accept affection and love. Parenting requires the firmness to set limits, the maturity to remain calm and centered, and the flexibility to meet the child's unique needs."

Notes... thoughts... questions to yourself

If you and your child need help developing a strong attachment, is there an experienced, well-trained attachment therapist nearby?

Attachment... living with reactive attachment disorder

LIVING WITH ATTACHMENT DISORDER
A First-Hand Account

We had struggles from her second day home. Hitting, kicking, biting, spitting, screaming, throwing, and more. For a long time, I attributed it to adjustment. Then to post-institutionalism, then to strong will. Her violence was almost always directed at me, and I spent many of my days covered in bite marks and bruises.

In addition to her violence toward me, she was extremely defiant, often refusing to do chores or even normal daily activities such as getting dressed or brushing her teeth. She was also very subtlety controlling and manipulative. She would repeatedly "forget" to do her chores. She would seldom do a task properly and would need to be redirected over and over to complete the task. Justine also showed extreme rage and mystification when she was given consequences for her misbehaviors; she took zero responsibly for her actions and behaviors. When I read and reread all the information on attachment and RAD, Justine barely fit the various lists. Yes, she raged at me, but she was not cruel to animals, she was affectionate, she had friends, she did well in school, she didn't lie, she showed empathy, she had a conscience, and so on. I realized that she had attachment "issues," but I never considered RAD.

In the spring, her violence toward me escalated dramatically in frequency, intensity, and duration, along with her other misbehaviors. After speaking on the phone with many therapists who didn't "get it," I finally found our super wonderful attachment therapist. She diagnosed Justine with RAD and PTSD. It was an overwhelming diagnosis to hear.

Our therapist's first goal was to get Justine's violence toward me stopped. Then we worked on compliance from Justine. Then we worked on her grief. We continually worked with Justine to let go of her early survival skills of control and manipulation.

For Justine to heal, she needed an attachment therapist and my complete commitment to a new parenting approach. Just therapy without the day-to-day therapeutic parenting wasn't enough.

I had to re-train my brain. I had to (tried to) learn to keep out of Justine's manipulations. I was very consistent. I was very structured. In order to help her "get" cause and effect, I over-exaggerated the consequences for all infractions. As I expanded my knowledge of RAD behaviors, I became more and more aware of behaviors of Justine's that were motivated by her lack of attachment (RAD), whereas previously I thought they were just annoying childhood behaviors. Throughout it all, I worked hard to maintain a loving, nurturing environment between me and Justine. We snuggled, read together, drew on each other's backs, and wrote each other sweet notes.

The work Justine and I have done together has been intense, mind- numbing, challenging, and the hardest thing I've ever done in my life. But it's working! I have truly witnessed a miracle. Justine is healing... substantially and dramatically. Justine has not shown any violence toward me. She follows directions and accepts my authority. She trusts me and shows me that I can trust her, too. She has become even more loving and affectionate. She's finding peace inside herself. She can share honest emotions with me, using her words. Her love toward me feels different, softer, truer, warmer. Recently, Justine (age 9) began playing and cuddling with a new doll. She holds the doll. Changes the doll. Talks to the doll. Sings to the doll. Keeps the doll safe. And looks into the doll's eyes. In the past, Justine did not have the knowledge, ability, or empathy to love and care for a baby doll. Now she does."

- Justine's Mama

Notes... thoughts... questions to yourself

As you read this short, first-hand account of parenting a child with RAD, did you wonder if it was exaggerated at all? Did you remind yourself that even though it would be hard to parent a child with RAD, with the right treatment, they can heal?

Attachment... the essential link is more important to your child than school, friends, or after-school activities

CONCLUSION

As an adoptive parent or parent-to-be, you're educating yourself about attachment, the most important aspect of parenting your child. Your child's ability to attach is the most fundamental trait she needs to become a loving, confident, successful person.

When your child arrives home, her attachment ability may be strong and merely need to be redirected and shaped to her new life: like the old house with a solid foundation, in need of a few coats of paint. Or, your child's attachment may be shaky and in-need of additional interventions and some assistance from a therapist: like the old house that requires re-wiring and re-plastering. Or, your child's attachments may be weak and insecure and in-need of long-term attachment therapy and therapeutic parenting: like the old house that was built with a poor foundation and needs major reconstruction.

No matter where your child falls within the continuum of attachment, be aware of the need for you to create an environment conducive for attachment. Provide not only love, but all of the attachment assistance your child needs to become a respectful, responsible, fun-to-be-around child, and a productive, caring adult.

Attaching to Your Child: A Helpful Checklist

Whether your child is newly adopted, has mild attachment issues, or has been diagnosed with RAD, this parenting checklist will help strengthen the attachment between you and your child.

Rate yourself a 1, 2, or 3. Three (3) means you have completed it or do it correctly most of the time. Two (2) means you do it some of the time. One (1) means you haven't completed it or often forget to implement it. Copy this list and fill it out at least once a month. If your child isn't improving, ask yourself, are you truly being honest in your self-evaluation? Do you need to find an attachment therapist?

Action to Improve Attachment	1, 2, 3	Note to self
1. Ask questions instead of telling your child what to do. It provides fewer opportunities for them to refuse to cooperate.		
2. Catch your child doing something right at least		

twice a day.		
3. Walk away from many negative behaviors, i.e., when your child is trying to argue. It keeps you out of potential power struggles.		
4. Read *Building the Bonds of Attachment* by Dan Hughes. Written like a novel, this book provides insights into parenting a child or foster child with RAD.		
5. Keep a calm, quiet, even-toned voice so that your child doesn't feel like they are able to control you and your emotions.		
6. Listen to at least one *Love and Logic* CD per month. It will remind you of positive ways to communicate with your child, even when they're trying hard to annoy you.		
7. Give your child several hugs or kisses each day for no reason.		
8. Keep sarcasm out of your		

voice. It only fuels your child's low sense of self esteem.		
9. Keep angriness out of your voice. Anger makes your child feel like they're in control.		
10. Show sadness for your child's bad choices, instead of frustration, annoyance, or anger. This will increase their capacity for problem solving.		
11. Provide consequences, not punishment, for your child's poor choices.		
12. Look at consequences as a way to build back trust rather than as punishment.		
13. Only give consequences when your child is calmed down.		
14. Do things that make your child giggle or laugh.		
15. Let your child overhear you telling someone about something they did right		

16. Expand your child's world (choices, privileges) when they're having good days.		
17. Reduce your child's world (choices, privileges) when they're having bad days.		
18. Let them solve their own problems--don't fix everything for them. This will add to their self confidence.		
19. Ask your child to notice and explain their feelings. This will teach them to share and discuss their feelings as an alternative to acting them out.		
20. Let your child hear you using emotion words, i.e., I feel sad, I'm so happy, I was annoyed . . . Unless your child hears you using these words, they will not be motivated to share their own feelings.		

ATTACHMENT RESOURCES... BOOKS

The Connected Child: Bring Hope and Healing to Your Adoptive Family
by Karyn B. Purvis, David R. Cross, and Wendy Lyons Sunshine, 2007

Parenting the Hurt Child: Helping Adoptive Families Heal and Grow
by G. C. Keck and R.M. Kupecky, 2009

Building the Bonds of Attachment
by Daniel A. Hughes, 2006

Attaching in Adoption: Practical Tools for Today's Parents
by Deborah D. Gray, 2012

Parenting with Love and Logic
by Foster Cline and Jim Fay, 2006

When Love Is Not Enough: A Guide to Parenting Children With RAD
by Nancy L. Thomas, 2005

ATTACHMENT RESOURCES... ONLINE

Love and Logic Institute
www.loveandlogic.com

Child Trauma Academy, Dr. Bruce Perry
www.childtrauma.org

Beatitude House Counseling Center
www.BeatitudeHouse.org

Association for Treatment & Training in the Attachment of Children
www.attach.org

Trauma Center: Bessel van der Kolk
www.traumacenter.org

Nancy Thomas Parenting
www.attachment.org

Attachment Disorder Maryland
www.attachmentdisordermaryland.com

CPSIA information can be obtained
at www.ICGtesting.com
Printed in the USA
LVHW091629030619
619978LV00039B/1293/P